For exams in 2022

ICAEW
Financial Management

GW01144617

TP06-7022-073

First edition 2007, Fifteenth edition 2021

ISBN 9781 5097 3891 5

British Library Cataloguing-in-Publication Data

A catalogue record for this publication is available from the British Library

Published by

BPP Learning Media Ltd
BPP House, Aldine Place
142–144 Uxbridge Road
London W12 8AA

www.bpp.com/learningmedia

Printed in the United Kingdom

Welcome to BPP Learning Media's **Passcards** for ICAEW **Financial Management**.

- They **save you time**. Important topics are summarised for you.

- They incorporate **diagrams** to kickstart your memory.

- They follow the overall **structure** of the ICAEW Workbook, but BPP Learning Media's ICAEW **Passcards** are not just a condensed book. Each card has been separately designed for clear presentation. Topics are self-contained and can be grasped visually.

- ICAEW **Passcards** are **just the right size** for pockets, briefcases and bags.

- ICAEW **Passcards focus on the exams** you will be facing.

Run through the **Passcards** as often as you can during your final revision period. The day before the exam, try to go through the **Passcards** again! You will then be well on your way to passing your exams.

Good luck!

Contents

1: Objectives

Topic List

Financial strategy

Stakeholders

Agency theory

This short chapter introduces the basic elements of financial strategy.

Investment decisions

Financing decisions

Risk management decisions

Risk management decisions

Specific techniques have been developed to mitigate the risk associated with investment and financing decisions.

These three types of decision cannot be taken in isolation from one another.

Investment decisions determine the way in which the organisation uses its financial resources. They always involve risk.

Financing decisions determine how the organisation obtains its financial resources and, in particular, the balance between its equity capital and its borrowings. Deciding the level of **dividends** is an important financial decision. Financing decisions also involve risk.

Ethical considerations

Ethical considerations pervade business decisions. The decisions involved in financial strategy are particularly susceptible to unethical practices. Those responsible for them must take care to avoid anything that might be considered to be dishonesty, misrepresentation, culpable negligence or even sharp practice.

Ethical considerations also include how decisions made by a firm impact on society and the environment. Firms need to take account of **sustainability** in their actions and decisions.

Sustainability in the context of the environment refers to carrying out actions whilst conserving the natural environment and minimising consumption of scarce natural resources.

Companies that consider their social and environmental impacts may end up improving shareholder wealth by having a positive effect on their economic performance.

A firm can take various measures to be sustainable such as:

- Minimising levels of waste and pollution
- Making better use of scarce natural resources
- Compliance with environmental legislation
- Controlling emissions
- Recycling

Many large multinationals inform stakeholders of how they are acting ethically in relation to the environment and society through voluntary sustainability reporting.

Stakeholders

Stakeholders are those that have a legitimate interest in the organisation's objectives.

The existence of multiple stakeholders can lead to multiple objectives – and conflicts between stakeholders.

Examples of stakeholders
■ Shareholders
■ Managers
■ Employees and unions
■ Lenders
■ Suppliers
■ Customers
■ Local community
■ Government and regulators

Role of shareholders

Ordinary (equity) shareholders are owners of the company, but the company is led by its board of directors.

Primary objective of companies

Maximisation of shareholder wealth

By focusing on this primary objective, clear decisions can be made.

However firms may attempt to **satisfice** – try to fulfil (partially) some stakeholder objectives, even if it means lower profits.

Agency theory

Individual team members act in their own self-interest, individual well-being depends on well-being of other individuals and team performance.

Agency theory and corporations

Corporations are owned by the principals (suppliers of finance) and run by the agents (management).

The agency problem

If managers don't have significant shareholdings, what stops them under-performing and over-rewarding themselves?

Sources of agency conflict

- Managers' success dependent on firm's success; shareholders diversify
- Managers short-term objectives; shareholders long-term
- Different risk attitudes
- Managers more hostile to takeovers as jobs threatened

Notes

2: Investment appraisal

Investment appraisal is an important aspect of financial management and accountants are expected not only to carry it out but to explain how they have reached their conclusions. Non-financial factors are likely to be very significant.

Payback

Is the time taken for the cash inflows from a capital investment project to equal the cash outflows, usually expressed in years.

It is used as a minimum target/first screening method.

Example

$'000	P	Q
Investment	60	60
Yr 1 profits	20	50
Yr 2 profits	30	20
Yr 3 profits	50	5

Q pays back first, but ultimately P's profits are higher on the same amount of investment.

Advantages

- ☑ Simple to calculate and understand
- ☑ Concentrates on short-term, less risky flows
- ☑ Can identify quick cash generators

Disadvantages

- ☒ Ignores timing of flows after payback period
- ☒ Ignores total project return
- ☒ Ignores time value of money
- ☒ Arbitrary choice of cut-off

Accounting rate of return

- Can be used to rank projects taking place over a number of years (using average profits and investment)

- Can also rank mutually exclusive projects

Method of calculation

$$\frac{\text{Estimated annual average profits}}{\text{Estimated average investment*}} \times 100\%$$

Where average investment =

$$\frac{\text{Initial outlay + scrap value}}{2}$$

Profit is **after** depreciation but before interest and taxation, ie, operating profit
* or initial investment

Advantages	Disadvantages
☑ Quick and simple calculation	☒ Takes no account of timing
☑ Easy to understand % return	☒ Based on accounting profits, not cash flows
☑ Looks at entire project life	☒ Relative, not absolute, measure
☑ Consistent with ROCE and EPS	☒ Ignores time value of money
☑ Uses balance sheet values	☒ Not consistent with wealth maximisation

Discounted cash flow analysis applies discounting arithmetic to the costs and benefits of an investment project, reducing value of future cash flows to present value equivalent.

Conventions of DCF analysis

- Cash flows incurred at beginning of project occur in year 0
- Cash flows occurring during time period assumed to occur at period-end
- Cash flows occurring at beginning of period assumed to occur at end of previous period

PV of cash flows in perpetuity

Annual cash flow/cost of capital

Discounting

Present value of $1 = \dfrac{1}{(1+r)^n}$

Annuity

Present value of annuity of $1 = \dfrac{1-(1+r)^{-n}}{r}$

r = discount rate
n = number of periods

Net present value (NPV)

Is the value obtained by discounting all cash flows of a project by a target rate of return/cost of capital. If NPV is positive, the project will be accepted, if negative it will be rejected.

Features of NPV

- Includes all cash flows related to project
- Allows for timing of cash flows
- Widely understood standard method

Example

=NPV(0.1,B2:F2)					
	A	B	C	D	E	F
1	Year	1	2	3	4	5
2	Cash flow £	20,000	20,000	20,000	20,000	30,000
3	NPV	82,025 (1)				
4	Initial investment	(80,000)				
5	Project NPV	2,025 (2)				

(1) This is the present value of the cash flows in cells B2 to F2 ie, for years 1–5. **The cash flow at the start of the first year is excluded** from this calculation because the formula assumes the first cash flow is **at the end of Year 1**.

(2) This is the project NPV **after subtracting the initial cash flows** at the **start** of Year 1.

| Investment appraisal techniques | Relevant costs and revenues | Tax and inflation | Replacement cycles and capital rationing | Shareholder value analysis | Foreign investment |

The IRR (internal rate of return) method calculates the rate of return at which the NPV is zero.

IRR Example

To calculate the IRR the correct instruction would be =**IRR(B2:G2)**.

=IRR(B2:G2)						
	A	B	C	D	E	F	G
1	Year	0	1	2	3	4	5
2	Cash flow £	(80,000)	20,000	20,000	20,000	20,000	30,000
3	IRR	11%					

Advantages of DCF methods

- ☑ Take into account time value of money
- ☑ Take account of all project's cash flows
- ☑ Allow for timing of cash flows
- ☑ Universally accepted methods

NPV

- Simpler to calculate
- Better for ranking mutually exclusive projects
- Easy to incorporate different discount rates

NPV and IRR comparison

For conventional cash flows when there is only one investment project (no mutually exclusive projects) both methods give the same decision

IRR

- More easily understood
- Can be confused with ROCE
- Ignores relative size of investments
- May be several IRRs if cash flows not conventional

NPV is widely accepted as the proper way to appraise investment opportunities.

Decisions should be based on relevant costs and revenues.

Relevant costs

The costs and revenues that are relevant to a decision are **future, incremental cash flows**.

Future, because no decision taken now can alter the past.

Incremental means directly traceable to the decision.

Cash flows because profit and loss are accounting concepts and introduce an extra layer of assumptions.

Non-relevant items

- **Sunk costs** – money already spent
- **Accounting entries with no cash flow impact** – eg, depreciation
- **Book values**
- **Committed or unavoidable costs**
- **Finance costs** – the finance decision is a separate issue (but see Chapter 6, adjusted present value)

Opportunity costs and revenues

All opportunity costs and revenues related to a project are relevant to it.

Opportunity cost of material
- Inventory in regular use – replacement cost
- Inventory with no other use – scrap value
- Material not in stock – purchase cost

Opportunity cost of labour
- Labour employed but currently idle – nil cost
- Labour currently working – labour cost plus contribution lost

Opportunity cost of using assets

Deprival value
lower of

Replacement cost   **Recoverable amount**
                          higher of

          Economic value   NRV

PV of cash generated by use of the asset

Taxation effects

Outflows

- Tax charged on net positive cash flows
- Unless the question says otherwise, assume:
  - Tax rate is 17%
  - Tax is paid at the end of the year to which it relates
  - Tax rate is constant over the life of the project

Inflows

- Tax relief is given on assets purchased by means of capital allowances ('writing down allowances' [WDA]). Assume WDAs at 18% reducing balance unless the question says otherwise
- No WDA in year of sale – balancing charge/allowance to reduce profit/loss to zero

Inflation

$$(1 + m) = (1 + r)(1 + i)$$

m = money rate; r = real rate; i = inflation rate

Money method

Discount cash flows incorporating inflation with the money rate. Use this method unless the question requires otherwise.

Real method

Remove effect of inflation from cash flows and discount using the real rate.

Effective method

Leave cash flows in t_0 terms and discount using effective rate (e).

$$1 + e = \frac{1+m}{1+i_s}$$

where i_s = inflation specific to given cash flow

Replacement cycles

- **LCM method** – evaluate costs over sufficient cycles of each length to make total times equal
- **Equivalent annual cost** – calculate PVs of replacement cycle options in the normal way, then divide by appropriate **annuity factor** to give **equivalent annual costs** for comparison

Other considerations in replacement analysis

- Changing technology/difficulty of exact replacement
- Inflation effects on eg, running costs, disposal revenue. If inflation affects all variables equally, use **real method** given above
- Taxation

Capital rationing

- **Hard rationing** – imposed by external capital markets
- **Soft rationing** – imposed by internal management policy
- **Syllabus is limited** to single period rationing, ie, shortage of funds at t0
- **Basic technique** – calculate profitability index (PI) (NPV per £ capital outlay) and rank projects
- **Divisible projects** – invest in projects in descending order of PI until funds all used
- **Indivisible projects** – trial and error to find feasible combination of projects with highest NPV
- **Mutually exclusive projects** – combine techniques above to satisfy all requirements
- **Project synergy** – consider mutually supporting projects separately and as single project, applying techniques as above

A shareholder value approach to performance measurement moves the focus away from short term profits to a longer term view of value creation.

Different shareholders will value different aspects of performance, although they will generally prioritise **financial returns**.

Rappaport's seven value drivers

- Sales growth
- Operating margin
- Fixed capital investment
- Working capital investment
- Cash taxes
- The planning period
- The cost of capital

All driving cash generation

Shareholder value = (business value – debt)

Where business value equals PV of free cashflows from operations plus the value of any marketable assets.

Real options

The value of the strategic options provided by a project may lead to its adoption even if its NPV is low or negative.

Real options
- Follow on options
- Abandonment options
- Timing options
- Growth options
- Flexibility options

Three important factors affecting market entry decisions:

- **Market attractiveness**
- Potential to achieve **competitive advantage**
- **Risk**

Cultural factors

- Business methods and practices
- Attitude to product features
- Prestige of investing company's own national culture

Financing factors

- Finance costs and subsidies
- Taxation
- Remittance of profits
- Access to local capital
- Parent/subsidiary repayment flexibility

Political risk

Possible hostile government action

Quotas, tariffs, non-tariff barriers, restrictions on action, minimum shareholding rules, nationalisation.

Assessing risk – consider:

- Government stability
- Political and business ethics
- Economic stability
- Past hostile action
- Extent of international indebtedness

Dealing with political risk

- **Negotiation** with host government and cultivation of good relationships
- **Insurance** eg, ECGD
- **Production strategy**: outsourcing, location of production facilities, enforceability of intellectual property rights
- **Structure**: joint ventures, licences, agencies

3: Risk and decision making

This chapter is concerned with investment risk and some of the techniques that can be used to manage it in a rational fashion. This is an important topic since risk is a constant feature of business decisions.

Business decisions are made without perfect knowledge of the future, so their outcomes are subject to **risk** and **uncertainty**.

Risk

A quantification of the potential variability in an outcome, based on past data, ie, probability-based techniques may be used.

Uncertainty

A unquantifiable degree of potential variability in an outcome, ie, probability theory provides no help.

Most people are **risk-averse**, in that they prefer low risks to high risk and uncertainty. Investors will expect the potential **reward** from a course of action to be **commensurate** with the degree of **risk** it entails

Decision making techniques for conditions of risk and uncertainty

Risk	
■ Probability distributions	■ Portfolio theory
■ Expected values	■ CAPM
■ Simulation	■ Risk adjusted discount rates

Uncertainty	
■ Minimum payback period	■ Prudent estimation
■ Use of higher discount rate	■ Best and worst case analysis
	■ Sensitivity analysis

Expected value

Expected value of a range of possible outcomes is the arithmetical mean of the outcomes weighted by their respective probabilities.

Expected values and other techniques

Expected values may be used with outcomes that combine the possibilities of more than one event using probability trees and payoff tables.

Strengths
☑ Information reduced to single outcome for each choice
☑ Idea of an average is readily understood

Weaknesses
☒ Probabilities relate to the long run and don't forecast the outcome of single decision
☒ Ignores range of possible outcomes and hence risk
☒ Ignores unacceptability to investors of possibility of large unfavourable outcome

Sensitivity analysis

Calculate the % change needed in each uncertain element to reduce NPV to zero.

Or calculate the effect on NPV of an x% change in the value of each uncertain element.

Strengths
☑ Helps to identify critical factors that must be monitored closely
☑ Simple concept, easy to understand
☑ Presents information in a useful way

Monte Carlo simulation

Employs random numbers, used when combination of events and probabilities are complex. Mean of distribution of outcomes is expected value, dispersion indicates degree of risk.

Weaknesses
☒ Assumes factors will vary independently of one another
☒ Ignores probability of a given degree of change in a factor
☒ Does not indicate correct decision. Merely provides decision-maker with useful information

Predictive analytics

Predictive analytics uses historical and current data to create predictions about the future.

Examples of predictive analysis include the following:

- Linear regression models
- Decision trees
- Simulations

Prescriptive analytics

By combining the statistical tools utilised in predictive analytics with Artificial Intelligence and algorithms, prescriptive analytics software can be used to calculate the optimum outcome from a variety of business decisions.

For financial management, these could include the following:

- Capital rationing decisions
- Replacement analysis
- Identifying the optimal balance of finance

3: Risk and decision-making

Mean

The mean (or average) of a set of data is calculated by taking the sum of all the values and dividing by the number of values in the distribution.

Standard deviation

The average amount of variability in a data set, the standard deviation shows how far, on average, each result lies from the mean (or expected value). A high standard deviation indicates higher risk.

Coefficient of variation

The ratio of the standard deviation to the mean, calculated as (standard deviation ÷ mean) × 100. The higher the percentage, the wider the dispersion of data around the mean and therefore the greater the risk.

Portfolio principle

A portfolio of several, individually risky, independent investments is less risky overall than single risky investment.

Capital asset pricing model

Based on comparing the systematic risk of individual investments with risks of all shares in the market.

- Investors/companies require return in excess of risk-free rate
- Unsystematic risk can be diversified away and no premium is required for it
- Investors/companies require a higher return from investments where systematic risk is greater

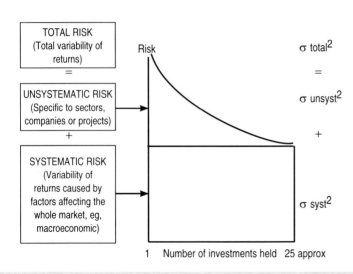

TOTAL RISK
(Total variability of returns)

=

UNSYSTEMATIC RISK
(Specific to sectors, companies or projects)

+

SYSTEMATIC RISK
(Variability of returns caused by factors affecting the whole market, eg, macroeconomic)

Risk

σ total^2

=

σ unsyst^2

+

σ syst^2

1   Number of investments held   25 approx

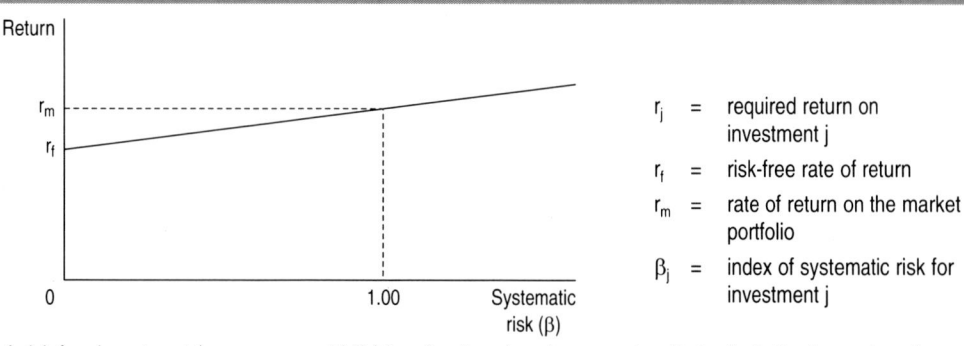

r_j = required return on investment j

r_f = risk-free rate of return

r_m = rate of return on the market portfolio

β_j = index of systematic risk for investment j

- A risk-free investment (eg, government bills) has $\beta = 0$ and produces a return that reflects the time value of money.
- The market portfolio has $\beta = 1.00$
- Individual securities' β values indicate the level of their systematic risk relative to the market portfolio.
- When the market rises, high β ('aggressive') securities will rise faster; the opposite is true of low β ('defensive') securities.
- The CAPM principle can be used to set risk-adjusted discount rates for capital investment projects; this assumes that shareholders have diversified portfolios.

The capital asset pricing model (CAPM) equation

can be used to calculate the required return on a security, and incorporates risk.

$$r_j = r_f + \beta_j (r_m - r_f)$$

where r_j is required rate of return on investment j

r_f is risk-free rate of return

r_m is the return on the market portfolio

β_j is beta factor for investment j (= index of systematic risk for security j)

Note that when applied to shares, r_j is the same as the cost of equity capital k_e (see Chapter 5 on cost of capital).

Beta factor (β)

measures the systematic risk of a security relative to the market.

Estimating beta for a new project must reflect business and financial (gearing) risk. Comparison with betas published for quoted companies may help.

Overall equity beta for a **diversified company** operating in different industry sectors will reflect the systematic risk of each sector.

Eg, a diversified company XYZ:

	Equity beta	% of total operation
Supermarket division	0.80	75%
Holiday division	1.10	25%

XYZ's overall equity beta = $(0.80 \times 75\%) + (1.10 \times 25\%) = 0.875$

Increasing risk

Beta < 1.0	Beta = 1.0	Beta > 1.0
Share < average risk	Share = average risk	Share > average risk
k_e < market average	k_e = market average	k_e > market average

Arbitrage pricing theory

The theory assumes that the return on each security is based on a number of independent factors.

$$r = E(r_j) + B_1 F_1 + B_2 F_2 \dots + e$$

Where $E(r_j)$ is expected return on security

B_1 is sensitivity to changes in Factor 1

F_1 is difference between Factor 1 actual and expected values

B_2 is sensitivity to changes in Factor 2

F_2 is difference between Factor 2 actual

e is a random term

Main problem – identifying macroeconomic factors and risk sensitivities.

Four-factor model

Other factors (than systematic risk) which are thought to affect the level of returns are:

- Size
- Value
- Momentum

Fundamental beta

This is a beta based on the basic notion of the risk-return relationship, ie, where a company's cash flows are subject to greater risk, the required return should be higher.

Notes

4: Sources of finance

This chapter provides some practical information on the problem of raising adequate capital. Linked to this is an introduction to international money markets and the efficient market hypothesis.

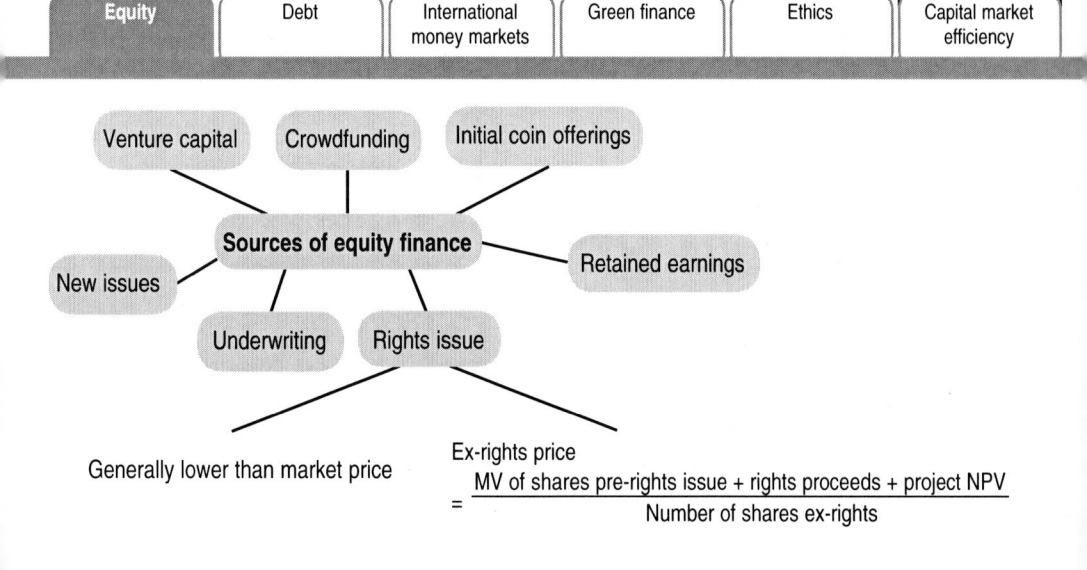

Venture capital

Crowdfunding

Initial coin offerings

Sources of equity finance

Retained earnings

New issues

Underwriting

Rights issue

Generally lower than market price

Ex-rights price

$$= \frac{\text{MV of shares pre-rights issue + rights proceeds + project NPV}}{\text{Number of shares ex-rights}}$$

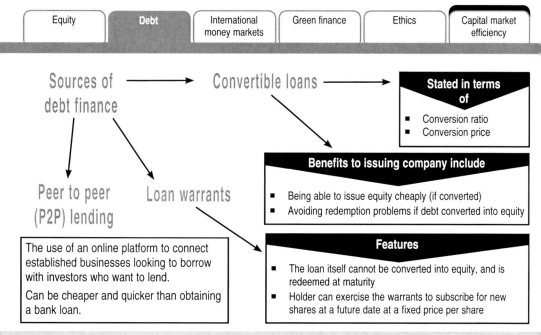

Sources of debt finance → Convertible loans →

Stated in terms of
- Conversion ratio
- Conversion price

Benefits to issuing company include
- Being able to issue equity cheaply (if converted)
- Avoiding redemption problems if debt converted into equity

Peer to peer (P2P) lending

Loan warrants

The use of an online platform to connect established businesses looking to borrow with investors who want to lend.

Can be cheaper and quicker than obtaining a bank loan.

Features
- The loan itself cannot be converted into equity, and is redeemed at maturity
- Holder can exercise the warrants to subscribe for new shares at a future date at a fixed price per share

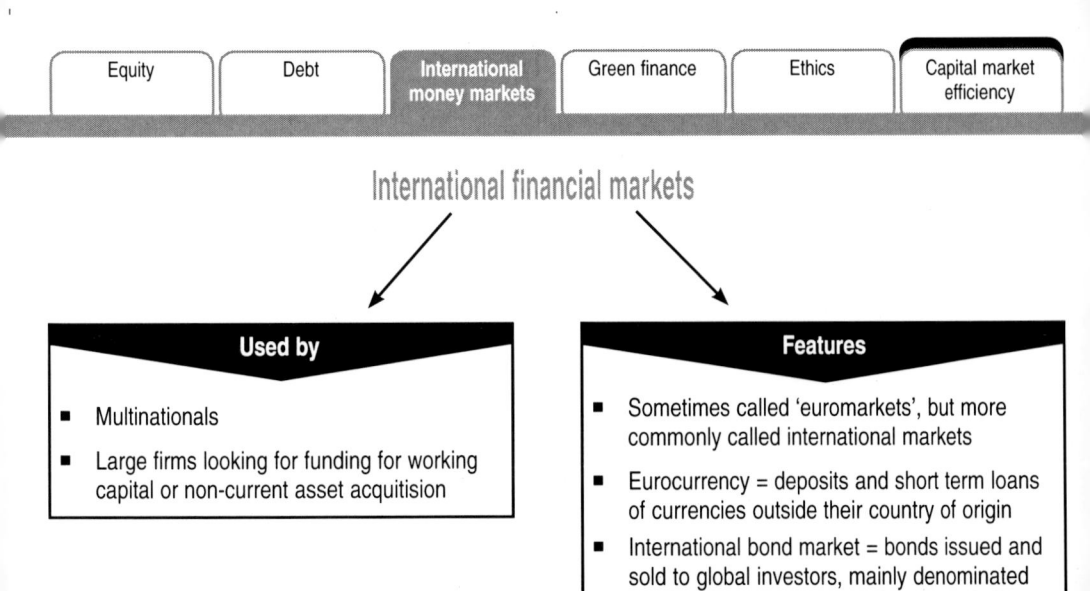

| Equity | Debt | **International money markets** | Green finance | Ethics | Capital market efficiency |

International financial markets

Used by

- Multinationals
- Large firms looking for funding for working capital or non-current asset acquitision

Features

- Sometimes called 'euromarkets', but more commonly called international markets
- Eurocurrency = deposits and short term loans of currencies outside their country of origin
- International bond market = bonds issued and sold to global investors, mainly denominated in US dollars, euros or yen; bonds traded internationally

The London Stock Exchange

- All member firms are broker-dealers, buying and selling securities on behalf of customers and on their own account

- Trade is carried out on computerised systems called SETS and SEAQ

- Market makers provide continuous buy and sell quotes in selected securities that trade frequently: this helps to create a liquid market in the securities

The efficient market hypothesis (EMH)

The prices in an efficient market reflect all relevant information. There are no opportunities to benefit by buying undervalued shares.

Weak form EMH
Share prices reflect information about past price movements

Semi-strong form EMH
Share prices reflect all publicly available information

Strong form EMH
Share prices reflect **all** information, whether published or not

Green finance

The financing of investments that provide environmental benefits.

Includes green crowdfunding for small-scale, community schemes or green bond issuance for major infrastructure projects.

Sources of green finance

Green loans – The provision of loans from banks specialising in financing green projects.

Green bonds – A type of fixed-interest bond used to raise money for climate and environmental projects. Often comes with tax incentives to enhance their attractiveness to investors.

ICAEW's **Code of Ethics** stresses the importance of the public interest, and of **public trust** in the profession. It sets out:

1 Fundamental principles
2 A conceptual framework
3 Threats to compliance
4 Safeguards

Fundamental principles

Integrity	Objectivity	Professional competence /due care	Confidentiality	Professional behaviour
✓ Straightforward ✓ Honest ✓ Fair ✓ Truthful ✗ Self-interest ✗ Undue influence ✗ Reckless ✗ False/misleading	✓ Independent of mind ✗ Bias ✗ Conflict of interest ✗ Undue influence	✓ Appropriate knowledge + skill ✓ Sound + independent judgement ✓ Diligence – careful, thorough, timely ✓ Technical/professional standards ✓ Distinction between expression of opinion + assertion of fact	✓ All unpublished information on employer/client is confidential ✓ Actively preserve confidentiality ✗ Disclosure ✗ Personal advantage	✓ Compliance with laws/ regulations ✓ Courtesy ✓ Consideration ✓ Honesty ✓ Truthfulness ✗ Actions that discredit profession ✗ Exaggerated claims ✗ Disparaging references to fellow professionals

Implications of the EMH

Weak form – technical analysis (chartism) provides no help in beating the market. Markets have no memory and past price movements offer no guidance about future prices, or when to issue new shares.

Semi-strong form – analysis of publicly available fundamentals makes the market semi-strong efficient but its effect on share prices is very rapid. Quoted firms cannot fool the market with window dressing since the market is concerned only with cash flows. Share prices are a better guide to performance than financial statements and ratio analysis.

Strong form – even insider dealing cannot beat the market.

Generally – in an efficient market prices are fair; investors will carry out their own portfolio diversification and will be unimpressed by conglomerate takeovers; new shares need not be issued at a discount so long as the risk and return are commensurate.

The stock exchanges of all developed nations are regarded as being at least semi-strongly efficient. This is linked to the amount of information quoted companies are required to provide to the markets.

Electronic share dealing platforms

Automatic trading is now extremely common and can lead to stock market volatility. The resulting volatility can reduce the efficiency of the stock market in terms of its ability to price shares accurately.

Behavioural finance

Behavioural finance is an alternative view to the efficient market hypothesis. It attempts to explain the market implications of the psychological factors behind investor decisions and suggests that irrational investor behaviour may significantly affect share price movements.

Some of the behavioural tendencies which can impact investor decisions are:

- Over confidence
- Representativeness
- Narrow framing
- Miscalculation of probabilities
- Conservatism

- Ambiguity aversion
- Positive feedback and extrapolative expectations
- Cognitive dissonance
- Availability bias

5: Cost of capital

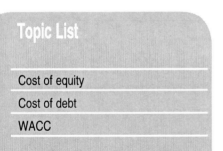

Topic List

Cost of equity

Cost of debt

WACC

Knowledge of cost of capital is needed for project appraisal and other financial management decisions. Generally, this will require consideration of both debt and equity, each of which has its own complicating factors.

Cost of equity if constant dividends paid

$$k_e = \frac{D_0}{P_0}$$

where: P_0 is ex-div price at time 0

D_0 is dividend

k_e is cost of equity or preference capital

Dividend growth model

$$k_e = \frac{D_0(1+g)}{P_0} + g = \frac{D_1}{P_0} + g$$

where: D_0 is dividend at time 0

D_1 is dividend at time 1

g is dividend growth rate

Estimating growth rate

Use experience or Gordon's growth model

$$g = rb$$

where: r is accounting return on opening capital employed

b is proportion of earnings retained

Problems with the Gordon model

- Relies on accounting profits
- Assumes r and b are constant
- Assumes all new finance is equity
- Effect of inflation

Shares have value
apart from dividends

Dividend growth rates
are not 0 or constant

Past not good guide
to future dividends

Problems of dividend valuation model

Share price used subject
to continual change

Level of earnings not
included in model

5: Cost of capital

The capital asset pricing model – CAPM (recap from Chapter 3)

Can be used to estimate the required return on a share and therefore the cost of equity capital of a company. CAPM incorporates **risk**.

$$r_j = r_f + \beta_j (r_m - r_f)$$

where: r_j is cost of equity capital/expected equity return

r_f is risk-free rate of return

r_m is return from market

β_j is beta factor of security

After tax cost of irredeemable debt capital

$$k_{dnet} = \frac{i(1-T)}{P_0}$$

where: k_{dnet} is the after-tax cost of the debt capital

i is the annual interest payment

P_0 is the current market price of the debt capital ex-interest

T is the rate of tax

Cost of convertible debt

1. Calculate value of conversion option
2. Compare conversion option and cash option
3. Calculate YTM of flows
4. Multiply by $(1-T)$

Cost of redeemable debt – IRR

Use the RATE spreadsheet function to calculate the pre-tax yield to maturity (YTM).

To calculate the RATE, the following variables need to be input to the RATE function.

=RATE(B1,B2,B3,B4)	
	A	B
1	Nper = the number of periods	X
2	Pmt = the amount (of interest) paid in any single period	X
3	Pval = the present value of the asset (its market price)	–X
4	Fval = the future value (the amount paid at maturity)	X
5	Yield to maturity	X

Post-tax K_d = Pre-tax K_d $(1-T)$

| Cost of equity | Cost of debt | WACC |

$$\text{WACC} = \frac{(MV_e \times k_e) + (MV_d \times k_d(I-T))}{MV_e + MV_d} = X \text{ times}$$

where: k_e is cost of equity
k_d is cost of debt

MV_e is market value of equity
MV_d is market value of debt

Use market values rather than book values unless market values unavailable.

Assumptions of WACC

- Project small relative to company and has same business risk as company
- Weights reflect company's long-term future capital structure and costs

Problems with WACC

- New investments may have different business risk
- New finance may change capital structure and perceived financial risk
- Cost of floating rate and bank loan capital not easy to calculate so take nominal value of bank loan and assume current interest rate is pre-tax cost of the loan

6: Capital structure and assessing financing options

Topic List

Capital structure theories

Other considerations

Project appraisal

Cash forecasts

Writing a business plan

This short chapter deals with the very important topic of capital structure. Both theoretical and practical considerations influence the extent to which a firm raises capital by borrowing and the chosen structure has important implications for project appraisal.

The production of cash budgets and forecast financial statements is an important practical aspect of planning and restructuring.

Risk and gearing

Business risk is the variability in the firm's EBIT caused by general conditions in the industry.

Financial risk is the additional variability in returns caused by financial gearing.

Operating gearing is the firm's ratio of fixed to variable operating costs.

Financing gearing is the firm's ratio of debt to equity measured in capital or income terms.

Capital: $\dfrac{\text{debt}}{\text{equity}}$ OR $\dfrac{\text{debt}}{\text{debt} + \text{equity}}$ **Income**: interest cover ratio

Traditional view of gearing

Initially, as debt is introduced into capital structure WACC falls because the premium required by shareholders to compensate for extra financial risk is more than compensated for by low cost of debt. However, as gearing increases to high levels, the risk premium required by shareholders increases and eventually WACC starts to rise. At very high gearing lenders become concerned about security and also start to require increased returns. Lowest WACC must be found by trial and error.

Traditional theory

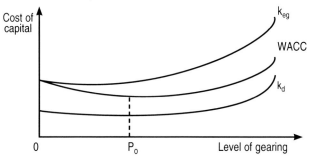

k_{eg}	is the cost of equity in the geared company
k_d	is the cost of debt
WACC	is the weighted average cost of capital
P_o	is the optimal capital structure where WACC is lowest

Assumptions

- All earnings paid out as dividends
- Earnings and business risk constant
- No issue costs
- Tax ignored

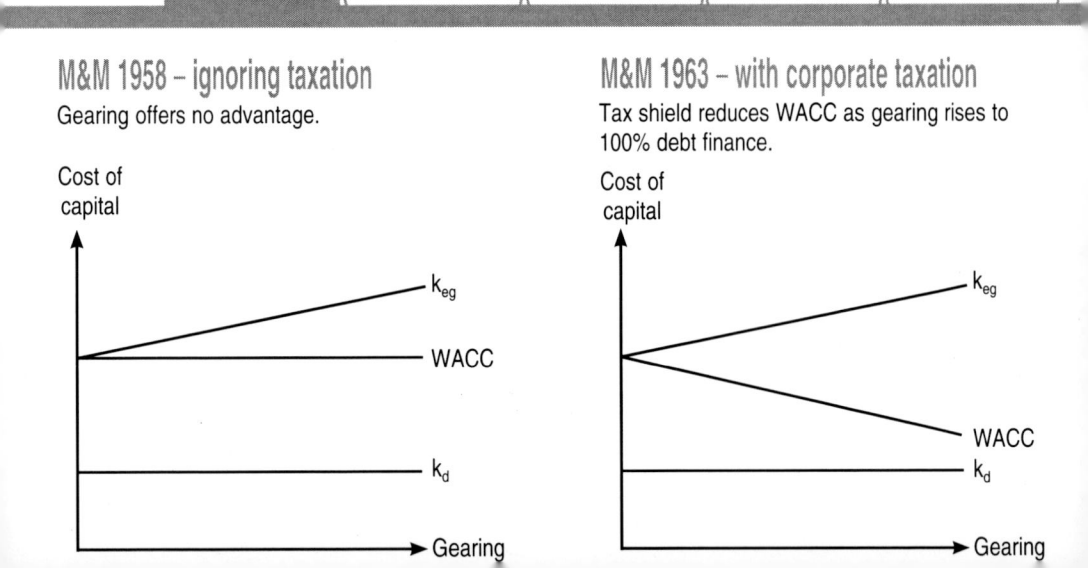

M&M 1958 – ignoring taxation

Gearing offers no advantage.

Cost of capital

k_{eg}

WACC

k_d

Gearing

M&M 1963 – with corporate taxation

Tax shield reduces WACC as gearing rises to 100% debt finance.

Cost of capital

k_{eg}

WACC

k_d

Gearing

Firms do not normally use a very highly-geared capital structure.

Bankruptcy costs – concern over possible default on interest can drive down MV of securities because of potential costs of liquidation, eg, redundancy, distress prices for assets.

Agency costs – the firm's directors could act against the interests of lenders who therefore impose debt covenants to control their activities. Compliance reduces freedom of action and imposes costs in terms of opportunities foregone.

Tax exhaustion – tax shield only applies if tax is payable. At high gearing, all tax allowances may be used up, removing tax shield effect of further borrowing.

Practical aspects

- **High business risk** may limit appetite for financial risk.
- **Substantial asset base** provides security for increased borrowing.
- Borrowing may be difficult for **small firms**.
- **Initial costs** vary between types of finance:
  Retained earnings – nil
  Equity issue costs – high
  Loan set up costs – moderate
- The higher the **tax rate** the higher the tax shield.
- **Signalling** – borrowing can communicate confidence on the part of directors and lenders.

Adjusted present value (APV)

When a firm considers financing a new project by increasing its borrowing, the project should be appraised using the new WACC as the discount rate. However, computing WACC requires knowledge of the market value of equity which depends on the PV of the project – which requires WACC for discounting.

Use of APV avoids this conundrum.

1. Calculate project PV using ungeared cost of equity as the discount rate (PV_1).

2. Calculate PV of tax savings from project borrowing (PV_2) using the pre-tax cost of debt as the discount rate.

3. Deduct any other costs, such as fees for arranging borrowing (C).

4. APV = $PV_1 + PV_2 - C$. Accept if APV is positive.

CAPM

As gearing increases, both cost of equity and equity beta (β_e) increase, because financial risk is systematic and cannot be diversified away.

Business assets suffer only systematic risk, measured by asset beta (β_a). This equals β_e in an ungeared firm, but as gearing increases, β_e increases, while β_a does not.

Assuming debt is risk-free:

$$\beta_e = \beta_a(1 + \frac{D(1-T)}{E})$$

where D and E are market values of debt and equity and T is the rate of corporation tax.

A **cash budget** may be prepared from detailed estimates of cash inflows and outflows, but there are **other methods**.

Forecast balance sheet
Individually identifiable items
- Bank loans
- Non-current creditors
- Issued capital
- Asset purchases and disposals
- Assume nil overdraft

Estimate using planning assumptions (eg, % growth)
- Inventory
- Receivables
- Payables
- Taxation
- Dividends
- Accum profit

$$\left\{ \begin{array}{l} \text{Share capital} \\ \text{and reserves} \end{array} \right. \begin{array}{c} > \\ (<) \end{array} \left\{ \begin{array}{l} \text{net} \\ \text{assets} \end{array} \right. = \begin{array}{l} \text{cash surplus} \\ \text{(cash deficit)} \end{array}$$

Forecast income statement and balance sheet

	£
Profit	X
(Increase)/decrease in inventory	X
(Increase)/decrease in receivables	X
Increase/(decrease) in payables	X
Operational cash flow	X̲

Changing conditions
- Basic **sensitivity analysis** techniques
- Changes in **economic variables** must be considered for their potential effect on demand
- Changes in **business variables** will also affect costs and revenues

Quality control of forecasts
- Regular review of variances
- Rolling updates

Funding cash deficiencies
- New share capital
- Additional borrowing
- Sale of short-term investments
- Delay payments to suppliers

The normal process of business planning will produce a range of documents such as financial forecasts; production and sales plans; and departmental budgets. These will probably deal with the long-, medium- and short-term in different degrees of detail. A business plan is often produced in detail as part of the process of raising funds from institutional investors. A business plan may include the following sections.

- **Preliminaries** — Title page, foreword, disclaimer, contents page
- **Executive summary** — Typically, a one-page summary of context and important material
- **History and background** — Origins; trading and technical development; goals; strengths and weaknesses; context for decisions
- **Mission and objectives** — Long-term aspiration and vision; shorter-term business goals; consider Ashridge four point mission statement
- **Products and services** — Current products and services offered; planned future developments; any unique selling proposition
- **Markets** — Nature of customers, including demographics, location, buying processes; quality level provided; competitor products and activity; current and expected market developments; distribution, pricing and promotion

■ **Resources, management and operations**	Key staff: CVs, organisation chart, job descriptions, succession plan Premises: location, tenure, size, facilities, costs Operations: broad description of activity and methods
■ **Financial information**	– Past and current revenue, costs, profitability and cash flows – Risk appraisal and management – Amount, purpose and timing of finance required – The offer to equity investors including exit route – Anticipated gearing – Sales, revenue and cash flow forecasts by month for the first year – Forecast financial statements by quarter or annually for up to five years – Supporting financial analysis: sensitivity; breakeven; basis of project appraisal (eg, discount rate, payback hurdle); set up costs for new venture or activity
■ **Action plan**	Detailed statement of main actions needed to execute the plan
■ **Appendices**	Detailed technical information such as:

– Product specifications	– Market research data
– Three years' audited financial statements	– Details of professional advisers

Notes

7: Equity sources and dividend policy

An understanding of what constitutes shareholder wealth is fundamental to deciding financial policy. Theory has some guidance to offer, but there are also some practical considerations.

M&M – the classic view

The cost of equity is the return required on equity funds no matter what their source since all equity funds contribute to shareholder wealth. Thus the cost of using retained funds is the same as the cost of newly-raised funds (issue costs are a separate matter).

Pricing new issues of shares

New issues are normally priced at less than market value in order to ensure that the issue is fully taken up. However, this may be to the detriment of existing shareholders.

Pecking order theory

The relative costs of new issues and rights issues leads to the idea of a 'pecking order' for equity funds determined by the costs involved in raising them.

1 **Retained earnings** involve no issue costs. However, their use can reduce the firm's ability to pay dividends which may cause market price to fall, thereby driving up the cost of equity.

2 **Rights issues** have relatively low issue costs.

3 **New public issues** tend to be the most expensive way to raise new equity finance.

M&M say that the pattern of dividend payments is irrelevant to determining shareholder wealth. A firm should invest in all available positive NPV projects; this will maximise shareholder wealth. Only when there is no available positive NPV project should dividends be paid.

Arguments against the M&M position

- A **dividend now is more certain** than a project extending into the future. This argument is fallacious since risk is not associated with time but with project conditions.

- **Dividends are important signals** to the market. An unpredictable and irregular flow of dividends will undermine share price. If true, this is an argument against the strong form of the EMH, since the dividend decision conveys information about a pre-existing state of affairs.

Other considerations

- **Clientele**
  Investors may have preferences for dividends or capital growth and may invest on that basis. This implies that sudden, large changes in dividend policy may adversely affect share price. Several factors may affect preference:
  - Investor's income/capital gain tax position
  - Need for cash, which is further affected by brokerage costs of realising shares
  - Need for capital growth in order to meet expected expansion in future liabilities

- **Agency theory**
  Generally, directors have discretion not to pay dividends and to invest retained profit. If they pay out any surplus in dividends, they will have to issue more shares to raise capital for further investment. This requires them to justify their plans and gives shareholders an effective veto.

Share buy-back

- Buy-backs allow companies to pay surplus cash to shareholders without disturbing the pattern of normal dividends, which might raise market expectations.
- Buy-backs are subject to the provisions of the Companies Act and Stock Exchange rules.

Scrip dividends

- A scrip dividend is a free issue of shares in proportion to current holdings instead of cash, thus protecting company liquidity.
- This has no effect on total shareholder wealth but substitutes capital gain for income.
- May be offered as alternative to cash dividend.
- If some shareholders take scrip and some take cash and company MV is affected, wealth will be transferred from one group to the other.

Conclusions on dividend policy

- Share value and dividend policy do not seem to be closely related.
- Clientele considerations (see above) are important.
- Stability of dividends is more important than their level.
- Many firms opt for stability, with slowly rising, regularly paid moderate dividends, while retaining sufficient earnings to permit a proper level of investment. This approach also allows the dividend to be maintained if there is a temporary fall in earnings.
- Exceptionally high earnings or a lack of investment opportunities may lead to share buy-backs or **special dividends**.

8: Business valuation

This chapter draws together several diverse topics linked to the fields of business valuation.

Organic growth

- Common option for start-up businesses since relatively undemanding of capital
- Spreads costs of growth over time
- Avoids disruption to systems, practices and culture common with acquisition
- If growth is by entry into a new but established market, organic growth more risky than acquisition of existing business
- Organic growth is slow
- Firm may fail to exploit available opportunities that would be available through takeovers
- Barriers to entry in new markets

Acquisition

- Allows rapid growth
- Can overcome barriers to entry
- Can reduce risk via portfolio effect, thus reducing cost of capital
- Can achieve synergy if systems, markets and assets fit well together
- Can reduce competition
- Vertical integration can capture more of the value in the supply chain and safeguard the current strategy
- Maximum price for target

  = MV of combined business – MV of bidder before bid made
- Using P/E: business value = P/E $\times$ earnings

Paying for an acquisition

- **Cash** – requires liquid funds but attractive to seller, though there may be tax implications

- **Share exchange** – preserves liquidity but dilutes existing shareholdings. Seller receives uncertain amount, incurs dealing costs and may have tax issue

- **Loan stock for shares** – avoids share dilution but affects gearing. More assured return for seller

Reasons for valuation

- Establish merger/takeover terms
- Enable share purchase/sale decisions
- Value companies listed on Stock Exchange
- Value shares sold in a private company
- Tax purposes
- Divorce settlements, etc
- Value subsidiaries for disposals, MBOs, etc

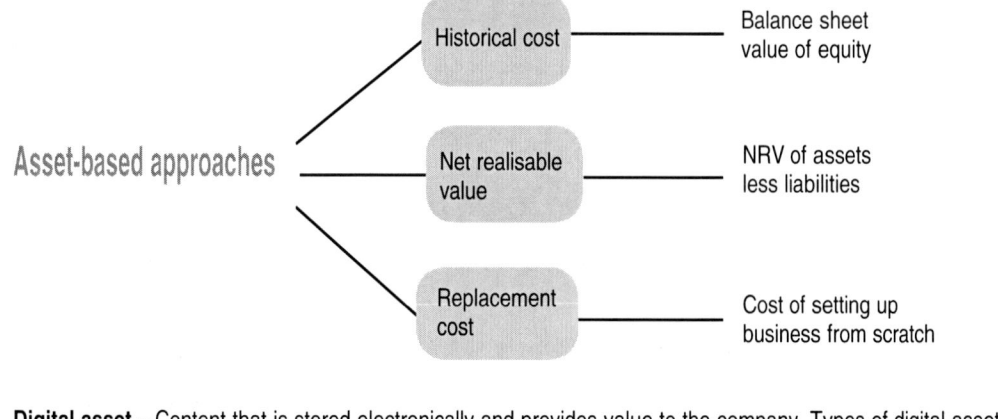

Digital asset – Content that is stored electronically and provides value to the company. Types of digital assets include photos, audio-visual media, spreadsheets, word documents, websites, and Big Data eg, information on customer behaviour.

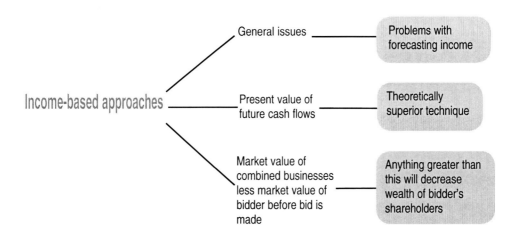

Income-based approaches

General issues —————— Problems with forecasting income

Present value of future cash flows —————— Theoretically superior technique

Market value of combined businesses less market value of bidder before bid is made —————— Anything greater than this will decrease wealth of bidder's shareholders

Price-Earnings (P/E) ratio

$$P/E\ ratio = \frac{Share\ Price}{Earnings\ per\ share\ (EPS)}$$

High P/E ratio tends to indicate high degree of investor confidence in company's future prospects.

Value of company using P/E ratio

Value = P/E ratio × Earnings

Problems with using P/E for company valuation

- Trying to estimate future earnings
- Figures can be manipulated by different accounting policies
- Selecting a suitable P/E ratio

Other income-based approaches include the **Enterprise value/EBITDA multiple, dividend valuation** and **SVA valuation**

1. **Enterprise value/EBITDA multiple:** enterprise value (EV) of the company divided by earnings before interest, tax, depreciation and amortisation.

   Often used in conjunction with, or as an alternative to, the P/E ratio.

   Enterprise Value Multiple $= \dfrac{\text{Enterprise Value}}{\text{EBITDA}}$

   EV = Mkt. Cap of equity + Preference shares + Debt − Cash and cash equivalents

2. **Dividend valuation method**

   $\text{Value} = \dfrac{d_0(1+g)}{(k_e - g)}$

   Where d_0 is the dividend at time 0

   g is the expected annual growth rate in future dividends

   k_e is the cost of equity

3. **Shareholder value analysis** – company valuation can be obtained through forecasting future free cash flows using the seven value drivers (Chapter 2)

4. **Valuation of technology companies** – Valuing start-up and technology companies is complicated by periodic swings in stock market sentiment (herd behaviour) that may result in over-valuation of these companies. The DCF approach is likely to be the most valid approach. Cash flows should be discounted at a risk-adjusted cost of capital.

Reasons for divestment

- **Lack of fit** with other business units
- Requires disproportionate **management time**
- **Conglomerate discount** – market sees current structure as counter-productive
- Poor trading results
- Release cash for other purposes
- Asset stripping
- Portfolio management by holding company

Management buy-out (MBO)

- A subsidiary or business unit is bought from the parent company by its existing management

- Buyers often need finance for a very large part of the purchase price. This is often a mixture of bank debt and venture capital debt and equity

- **Junk bonds** are high risk, high cost

- **Mezzanine** debt finance is made cheaper by including either an option to convert to equity or warrants giving a right to buy equity

- **Management buy-in** is similar except that the purchasing management group are external to the business

Sell-off

Normally a cash sale of part of a business to another established business.

Winding-up

- Often enforced by creditors but may be undertaken by shareholders to realise assets if business purpose has come to an end

- Value as going concern is important consideration

Share buy-back

- Can enhance share price by reducing supply. EPS will increase if cash used for buy-back was not previously earning an adequate return
- Provides an exit route for shareholders in unquoted companies
- Can be used to increase gearing ratio

Spin-off or demerger

- Part of an existing business is established as a separate corporate entity. Shares are then distributed to the owners of the parent company in proportion to their existing holdings
- Can overcome **conglomerate discount** (see above)
- Can be used to prevent a takeover of the whole company by spinning off the most attractive part
- Ownership is unchanged – shareholders can decide whether to sell or not

Outsourcing

- Goods and services needed by the business are brought in rather than produced internally. Can involve running down some business functions such as HR and distribution
- Allows firm to benefit from supplier's scale economies and specialist skills
- Firm concentrates its resources on its value-producing core activities
- May present problems of control and quality

9: Managing financial risk: interest rate and other risks

Derivatives are sophisticated financial products that are widely used as a kind of insurance against downside market risk. Like ordinary insurance, they are based on the transfer of risk to a third party in return for the payment of a premium. An important exception to this general model is the interest rate swap, which is an application of the principle of comparative advantage.

Terms

A **financial derivative** is a financial instrument whose value is derived from the value and characteristics of an underlying financial item.

A **forward contract** sets a binding price today, for an item to be delivered at a set future date. A forward contract is arranged over the counter to the specific requirements of the customer.

A **future** is an exchange-traded standardised contract to buy or sell a specific amount of a commodity, currency or financial instrument at a particular price at a set future date.

An **index future** can be used to hedge against a fall in value of a share portfolio.

Futures do not provide a perfect hedge; their use will always impose a cost, for two reasons:

- The value being hedged must be rounded to a whole number of contracts
- **Basis**, which is the difference between spot and futures price on a given day

Apart from these effects, futures operate to remove both upside and downside risk.

An **option** is an agreement giving the buyer the right, but not the obligation, to buy or to sell a specific quantity of something (eg, shares, currency, a commodity) at a known or determinable price (exercise price, strike price) within a stated period. Purchase of an option removes downside risk at the cost of the purchase price of the option (the **premium**).

Terminology

- A **negotiated** or **over-the-counter** option is tailor-made for specific needs
- **Traded options** are standardised
  - **American style** – may be exercised on any day until the expiry date
  - **European style** – may be exercised only on the expiry date
- **Call/put** option – the purchaser of the option has the right to **buy/sell** the underlying asset
- Options are **written** by **option writers**, typically large financial institution
- An option that would make a profit/make a loss/break even if exercised today i**s in/out of/at the money**
- **Index option**s are based on (eg,) the FTSE100 share index. Contract size is a notional index value multiplied by £10 (eg, 6,000 × £10 = £60,000 contract size). Exercise prices are available at intervals of 50 index points (eg, 5,900, 5,950, 6,000, 6,050, 6,100). Index options are used to hedge against adverse movements in the market overall and for speculation.

Valuing options

Intrinsic value – based on the assumption that the option expires today.

- **Call option** – the higher of (1) underlying asset price minus exercise price and (2) zero
- **Put option** – the higher of (1) exercise price minus underlying asset price and (2) zero

Time value

Actual quoted option prices are always higher than their intrinsic value (except on expiry date for the option): the difference is **time value** or **time premium**.

- Time value falls as the time to expiry reduces
- Time value tends to increase with underlying asset spot price variability – the more volatile the spot price, the greater the chance of the option being in the money
- Time value depends on the general level of interest rates, since exercise will be at some future time and the value of the option depends on the present value of the future exercise price. The higher/lower the discount rate, the lower/higher the PV.

Interest rate risk

Fixed v floating rate debt   Change in interest rates may make borrowing option chosen the less attractive option

Currency of debt   Effect of adverse movements if borrow in another currency

Term of loan   Having to re-pay loan at time when funds not available => need for new loan at higher interest rate

Forward rate agreement

An FRA means that the interest rate will be fixed at a certain time in the future. Loans > £500,000, period < 1 year. Fixed interest rates reflect banks' expectations for future interest rate changes.

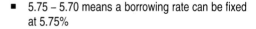

- 5.75 – 5.70 means a borrowing rate can be fixed at 5.75%

- '3 – 9' FRA is for an interest period starting in three months and lasting for six months

- Basis point is 0.01%

Interest rate futures

Hedge against interest rate movements. The terms, amounts and periods are standardised. Three months is the standard period.

- The futures prices will vary with changes in interest rates
- Outlay to buy futures is less than buying the financial instrument
- Price of short-term interest rate futures (STIRs) quoted at discount to 100 per value (93.40 indicates deposit trading at 6.6%)
- STIR is a future on a three-month deposit of a standard amount. A borrower wishing to hedge risk of future increase in the interest rate will sell futures

Maturity mismatch

Occurs if the actual loan period does not match the notional contract length (three months). The period of the loan determines how many futures contracts are needed.

Number of contracts =

$$\frac{\text{Size of exposure (eg, loan) to be hedged} \times \text{Interest period to be hedged}}{\text{Futures contract standard size} \times \text{Standard contract duration}}$$

Interest rate option

> Grants the buyer the right, but not the obligation, to deal at an agreed interest rate at a future maturity date.

- If a company needs to hedge **borrowing, purchase put options**
- If a company needs to hedge **lending, purchase call options**

To calculate effect of options, use same proforma as currency options.

Example below shows premiums for options on interest rate futures

Strike price	Calls			Puts		
	Nov	Dec	Jan	Nov	Dec	Jan
96.00	0.87	1.27	1.34	0.29	0.69	1.06

- Strike price is price paid for futures contract
- Numbers under each month represent premium paid for options
- Put options more expensive than call as interest rates predicted to rise

Interest rate swaps

Are agreements where parties exchange interest commitments. In simplest form, two parties swap interest with different characteristics. Each party borrows in market in which it has **comparative advantage**.

Uses of interest rate swaps

- Switching from floating rate to fixed interest
- Raising less expensive loans
- Securing better deposit rates
- Managing interest rate risk
- Avoiding charges for loan termination

Example

SONIA currently 8%. Co A has a fixed rate loan but wants floating rate: best available is SONIA + 2%. Co B has floating rate loan but wants fixed rate: best available is 10%. Swap benefits both parties.

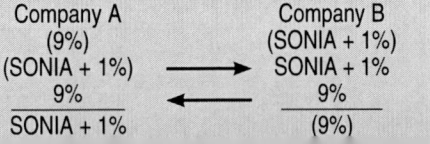

	Company A	Company B
Interest paid on loan	(9%)	(SONIA + 1%)
A pays to B	(SONIA + 1%) →	SONIA + 1%
B pays to A	9% ←	9%
	SONIA + 1%	(9%)

Risks

- **Counterparty** default
- **Market risk** – unfavourable market rate movements may occur
- **Transparency risk** – potential for misleading financial statements

10: Managing financial risk: overseas trade

Foreign trade brings its own particular risks. Many of these arise from political, economic and cultural factors. Foreign currency exchange has its own risks and a variety of methods is available for hedging against them.

Quoting exchange rates

Spot rate is the exchange rate offered for immediate delivery.

Forward rate is the exchange rate offered for exchange at a pre-determined future date.

Dealers offer a **buying rate** and a **selling rate** (**bid** and **offer** rates). The **mid-point** is often quoted as the exchange rate, but no trading is done at this rate.

A **direct quote** gives the amount of domestic currency that is exchangeable for one foreign currency unit.

An **indirect quote** gives the amount of foreign currency that is exchangeable for one domestic currency unit. Indirect quotes are always used for sterling but direct quotes are more common in most other countries.

Currency risk

Transaction risk is the risk of adverse exchange rate movements during normal international trading transactions. This is the main concern of exchange risk management.

Translation risk is the risk of reporting a loss when the accounting results of foreign branches are translated into domestic currency values.

Economic risk is the risk that exchange rate movements may degrade a company's international competitiveness. This kind of risk can only be managed by diversification of suppliers and markets.

Should we hedge?

- Cost
- Exposure
- Overall attitude to risk
- Portfolio effect of firm's international trade
- Shareholders' own portfolio effect
- Effect on cost of capital of reducing insolvency risk

Direct risk reduction methods

Invoice currency

Both suppliers and customers may seek to avoid transaction risk by having invoices denominated in their own domestic currency. The party who pays or receives foreign currency suffers the risk.

Matching receipts and payments

Foreign currency receipts may be held in a bank account denominated in that currency and used to make payments in the same currency, thus making exchange rate movements irrelevant except for any net cash requirements or surplus to be exchanged.

Matching assets and liabilities

Future foreign currency receipts may be hedged by borrowing in the currency now and using the receipts to pay the loan. Similarly, future payments could be made from an account set up now. Foreign fixed assets may be financed by borrowing in the local currency.

Leads and lags

Firms may speculate in exchange rate movements by making payments early or late as appropriate but must also consider settlement discounts and finance costs.

Netting

Payments due on intra-group trade may be netted off so that actual currency flows are minimised. This may be bilateral or multilateral.

- Foreign exchange dealing costs (commission and bid-offer spread) are minimised.
- Less money is in transit and thus finance costs are reduced.

Forward exchange contract

- A firm and binding contract between a bank and its customer
- For the purchase/sale of a specified quantity of a stated foreign currency
- At a rate fixed at the time the contract is made
- For performance at a future time agreed when contract is made
- Forward rates are derived from spot rates and money market interest rates. They are not a prediction of what the spot rate will be at a future time

Forward rates as adjustments to spot rates

Forward rate cheaper   –   Quoted at **discount**

Forward rate more expensive   –   Quoted at **premium**

Add discounts, or **subtract premiums** from spot rate.

Purchasing power parity

Predicts that disequilibrium caused by different inflation rates in different companies will be removed by prices changing:

$$\frac{1 + \text{US inflation rate}}{1 + \text{US inflation rate}} = \frac{\text{US\$ / £ Fwd rate}}{\text{US\$ / £ Spot rate}}$$

Interest rate parity

Must hold between spot rates and forward rates (for the interest rate period), otherwise arbitrage profits can be made:

$$\frac{1 + \text{US interest rate}}{1 + \text{US interest rate}} = \frac{\text{US\$ / £ Fwd rate}}{\text{US\$ / £ Spot rate}}$$

Currency futures

A **currency future** is a contract to buy or sell a standardised amount of a notional currency for notional delivery at a set date in the future.

Futures terminology

Closing out a futures contract means entering a second futures contract that reverses the effect of the first.

Contract size is the fixed minimum quantity that can be bought/sold eg, £62,500 in exchange for US dollars.

Contract price is in US dollars, eg, $/£ 1.4500.

Settlement date is the date when trading on a futures contract ceases and accounts are settled.

Basis risk is the risk that futures price movement may differ from underlying currency movement.

Advantages and disadvantages of futures contracts

Advantages

- ☑ Transaction costs lower than forward contracts
- ☑ Futures contract not closed out until cash receipt/ payment made

Disadvantages

- ☒ Cannot tailor to user's exact needs
- ☒ Only available in limited number of currencies
- ☒ Hedge inefficiencies

Cryptocurrency

Cryptocurrencies are computer files which owners can transfer to others electronically as a means of paying for goods and services. Bitcoin is the oldest and best-known cryptocurrency, a type of currency that does not have a physical form – it can be used to settle international transactions. Pricing risk can be hedged using derivatives such as futures.

Money market hedging

Future foreign currency payment	**Future foreign currency receipt**
1 Borrow now in home currency	**1** Borrow now in foreign currency
2 Convert home currency loan to foreign currency	**2** Convert foreign currency loan to home currency
3 Put foreign currency on deposit	**3** Put home currency on deposit
4 When have to make payment	**4** When cash received

(a) Make payment from deposit
    (b) Repay home currency borrowing
	(a) Take cash from deposit
	    (b) Repay foreign currency borrowing

Currency option

> Is a right, but not an obligation, to buy or sell currency at a stated rate of exchange at some time in the future.

Removes **downside** risk but retains upside potential.

Over the counter options are tailor-made options suited to a company's specific needs.

Traded options are contracts for standardised currency amounts, only available in certain currencies.

Useful when timing and amount of cash flows is uncertain.

- Support tender for overseas contract
- Allow publication of price lists in foreign currency
- Protect import/export of price-sensitive goods

Choosing the right option

UK company wishing to sell US dollars at a future date can purchase sterling traded call options on sterling (option to buy sterling = option to sell US dollars)

Drawbacks of options
■ Cost dependent on expected volatility
■ Pay on purchase
■ Tailor-made options are not negotiable
■ Traded options not in every currency

Options vs forwards and futures

- **Adverse currency movement**: option hedge not as good because of premium cost
- **Favourable currency movement**: option better, since need not be exercised, therefore option holder benefits from movement in the spot exchange rate

A **currency swap** is an interest rate swap in which the parties are borrowing in different currencies.

One of the parties is a bank that specialises in arranging swaps.

A currency swap is similar to an interest rate swap, except that interest payments are exchanged in different currencies (perhaps both a fixed rate) and there is an actual exchange of the principal amounts of the currencies at the end of the term of the swap.

Advantages	Risks
☑ **Hedging available where there is no market**, eg, for the longer term or in currencies where there is no market for other hedges	■ **Counterparty risk** – the counterparty may default on his agreed payments
☑ **Access to foreign debt markets**	■ **Position (market) risk** – the risk of unfavourable interest or exchange rate movements after the swap is set up
☑ **Translation risk** can provide a means of matching receipts and payments when trading in foreign countries	■ **Sovereign risk** – political disturbance or exchange controls in the foreign country
☑ **Interest rate swap** may be arranged as part of the deal, eg, to convert fixed to floating rate	■ **Transparency risk** – as for interest rate swaps
☑ **Liquidity** can be transferred from one currency to another	
☑ Can overcome **exchange controls**	

Economic exposure

The risk that longer-term exchange rate movements might reduce a company's international competitiveness.

Taken in isolation, exchange rate movements have obvious effects on the costs and revenues relating to international trade. However, economic influences are interlinked, often in complex ways and other effects may compensate for disadvantageous exchange rate movements. In particular, inflation is usually linked to both interest and exchange rates.

Hedging economic exposure

- Only possible in the **longer term**
- **World-wide diversification** of operations, costs and revenues
- **Marketing decisions** must consider economic exposure
    - Product launch risk may increase
    - Market entry must be carefully considered
    - Prices may have to respond to local factors as well as international ones

Translation risk

Translation risk is subject to **debate**:

- Losses and gains on translation do not represent cash flows, so may be ignored
- Accounting results will affect the share price, so translation losses should be minimised

Foreign trade risk

Foreign trade involves a greater degree of risk than domestic trade because of political and cultural factors and the extra distances and times involved.

Extra risks of foreign trade

- **Physical** – lost or stolen goods or documents
- **Credit** – payment default by customers
- **Trade** – order cancellation/refusal to accept goods
- **Liquidity** – can't finance the extra trade credit required

Some risks may be transferred, eg, to shipping companies or by means of insurance in various forms.

Reducing the risk of bad debts

- Normal credit control methods should be used
- **Bills of exchange**
  Bills of exchange are widely used in foreign trade. Banks may accept bills on behalf of an exporter or importer: a bank bill is effectively a guarantee of payment by the bank
- **Export factoring**
  Essentially the same as domestic factoring
- **Export credit insurance**
  Covers special risks of exporting

Documentary credits (letters of credit)

Give exporters a risk-free method of obtaining immediate payment (less discount for early settlement), subject to shipping the goods and compliance with terms of a letter of credit. Buyer obtains a period of credit.

Notes